First
Facts

Our Government

The U.S.
House of
Representatives

by Muriel L. Dubois

Consultant:
Steven S. Smith
Kate M. Gregg Professor of Social Sciences
Washington University, St. Louis, Missouri

Capstone
press

Mankato, Minnesota

First Facts is published by Capstone Press
151 Good Counsel Drive, P.O. Box 669, Mankato, Minnesota 56002
http://www.capstone-press.com

Library of Congress Cataloging-in-Publication Data
Dubois, Muriel L.
  The U.S. House of Representatives / by Muriel L. Dubois.
    p. cm. — (First facts. Our government)
    Summary: Introduces the United States House of Representatives and how a
bill becomes a law.
    Includes bibliographical references and index.
    ISBN 0-7368-2288-7 (hardcover)
    1. United States. Congress. House—Juvenile literature. 2. Legislators—United States—
    Juvenile literature. [1. United States. Congress. House. 2. Legislators. 3. Legislation. 4.
    United States—Politics and government.] I. Title. II. Series.
JK1319.D83 2004
328.73'072—dc21   2002155473

Editorial Credits
Christine Peterson, editor; Jennifer Schonborn, series and book designer; Jo Miller, photo
    researcher; Eric Kudalis, product planning editor

Photo Credits
AP/Wide World Photos, Dennis Cook, 8–9; Charles Bennett, 14–15
Corbis/AFP, 16
Folio Inc./Patricia Fisher, cover; Robert C. Shafer, 7
Getty Images/Mark Wilson, 11; REUTERS/ Win McNamee, 13; Kenneth Lambert, 19;
    Alex Wong, 20
Ophelia Lenz/Intelligencer, 5
Photri-Microstock, 17

1 2 3 4 5 6 08 07 06 05 04 03

Table of Contents

Children Learn about Voting

U.S. representatives pass laws for the country. They wrote a law to help children learn about voting. The law gives states money for Kids Voting USA. This group holds elections just for children. Children can vote for leaders, including members of the U.S. House of Representatives.

Fun Fact:
Children in 38 states are part of Kids Voting USA.

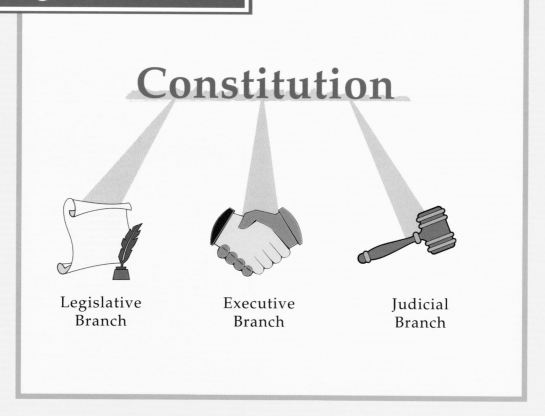

Constitution

Legislative
Branch

Executive
Branch

Judicial
Branch

The U.S. government has three parts. The
legislative branch writes laws. The executive
branch makes sure laws are being followed.
The judicial branch explains laws.

Congress is the legislative branch. The Senate and House of Representatives make up Congress. Together, they work in the Capitol in Washington, D.C., to pass new laws.

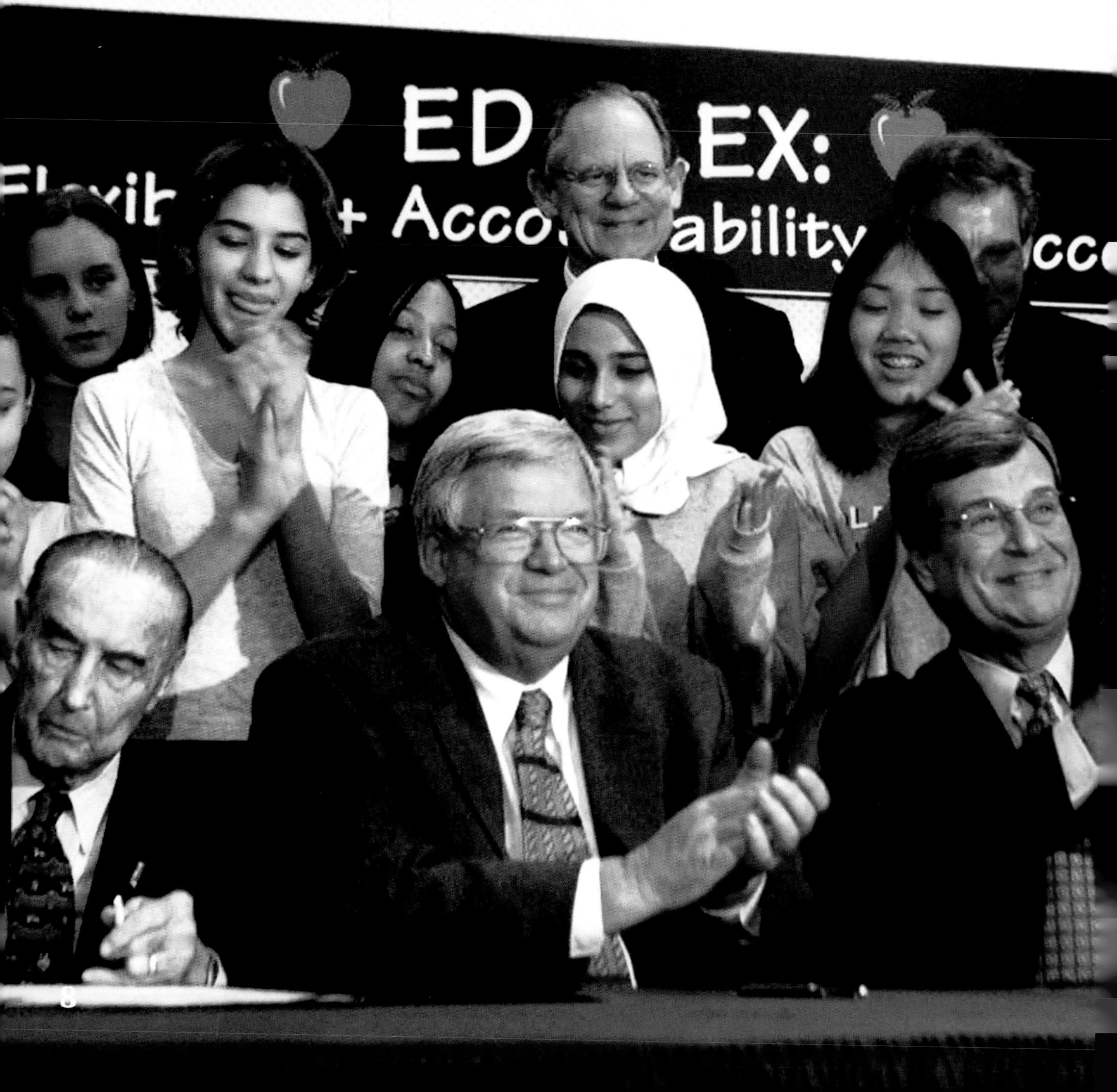
ED
EX:
+ Acco
ability

A Bill Becomes Law

Members of Congress write bills that may become laws. Ideas for new bills can come from the president, Congress, or citizens. Representatives talk about bills and then vote. If both the House and Senate pass a bill, it goes to the president. The president signs or vetoes the bill.

Fun Fact:
House members write and study more than 4,800 bills each year.

Who Can Be a Representative?

Representatives need to meet certain requirements. They need to be U.S. citizens for seven years or more. They must be at least 25 years old. They must live in the state where they are elected. Representatives serve for two years. They then can run for office again.

 **Fun Fact:**
Since 1917, more than 190 women have served in the U.S. House of Representatives.

11

Representatives Serve Many People

People in every state elect leaders to serve in the House of Representatives. The House has 435 members. States with many people have more representatives. Each representative works for their home state. They each serve thousands of people.

Fun Fact:
When the first Congress met in 1789, the House had 65 members.

A Representative's Job

Representatives have many duties. They meet with people of all ages to talk about the country. They study ideas and suggest bills. Representatives help set up taxes. They decide how tax money is spent.

14

A Representative's Day

Representatives go to meetings each day. Some days, they meet in small groups to talk about bills. Other days, they meet in a large group to vote on bills.

Representatives go to events at the Capitol.
They meet with other government leaders.
House members also visit with people from
their home state.

The Speaker of the House

The Speaker of the House is the leader of the U.S. House. Representatives elect the Speaker. The Speaker calls on members to talk about bills. The Speaker meets with the president and leaders of the Senate to talk about bills.

Fun Fact:
When representatives begin a new session, the first thing they do is vote for the Speaker of the House.

Amazing But True!

The Speaker of the House uses a plain wooden gavel to begin and end meetings. The gavel is also used to signal when representatives are about to vote. The gavel often breaks when the Speaker hits it on the desk. Extra gavels are kept nearby in case one breaks.

Hands On: Write a Bill

Write a bill for a new law in your state. Send your idea for a new bill to your U.S. representative.

What You Need

Pencil

Paper

Envelope

Postage stamp

An adult to help

What You Do

1. Think of an idea for a new law for your community.
2. Use a pencil to write your idea on a piece of paper. In Congress, all bills begin with, "For the establishment of" (the name of a law).
3. Explain why the bill is needed and how it will work.
4. Sign the bill.
5. More than one person can sign a new bill. Ask teachers, family members, or friends to sign your bill.
6. Put your bill in an envelope.
7. Put a postage stamp on the envelope's upper right corner.
8. Mail your bill to a U.S. representative. Ask an adult to help find the address of your U.S. representative at the official Internet site *http://www.house.gov*. Addresses for House members can also be found at local and school libraries.

Glossary

citizen (SIT-i-zuhn)—a member of a country who has a right to live there

executive (eg-ZEK-yuh-tiv)—the branch of government that makes sure laws are followed

judicial (joo-DISH-uhl)—the branch of government that explains laws

legislative (LEJ-iss-lay-tiv)—the branch of government that passes bills that become laws

representative (rep-ri-ZEN-tuh-tiv)—a person elected to serve the government

requirement (ri-KWIRE-muhnt)—something that you have or need to do

veto (VEE-toh)—the power or right to stop a bill from becoming a law

Read More

Fitzpatrick, Anne. *The Congress.* Let's Investigate. Mankato, Minn.: Creative Education, 2003.

Murphy, Patricia J. *The U.S. Congress.* Let's See Library. Our Nation. Minneapolis: Compass Point Books, 2002.

Sobel, Syl. *How the U.S. Government Works.* Hauppauge, N.Y.: Barron's, 1999.

Internet Sites

Do you want to find out more about the U.S. House of Representatives? Let FactHound, our fact-finding hound dog, do the research for you.

Here's how:
1) Go to **http://www.facthound.com**
2) Type in the **BOOK ID** number: **0736822887**
3) Click on **FETCH IT**.

FactHound will fetch Internet sites picked by our editors just for you!

Index